HAPPY VEGGIES

MAYUMI ODA

Do you want to meet Mother Nature?
Come into my vegetable garden.

Cabbages wake up early.
They open their leaves and begin to sing.

Spring warms the earth.
Asparagus poke their heads out.
Where were they hiding?

Dressed up, all in a line,
The Onion Family greets us.

"Fly up, fly up, Mighty Butterflies.
Enjoy our pollen."

Potatoes are a garden's heart.
Can you hear them? Thump. Thump. Thump.

From the dark earth,
Radishes and carrots are born.
The earth is their mother.

Sweet smells fill the herb garden.
Angels sometimes come to play.

Beans long to see the summer sky
Grow, grow!
Reaching for the heavens.

Tomatoes feast on the summer sun
'Til their bellies are full to bursting.

Dangle, dangle—
Cucumbers dangle,
Eggplants dangle.
The summer garden
Dangling vegetables.

Bees on blossoms
Buzzing away.
Little baby pumpkins
Get fatter every day.

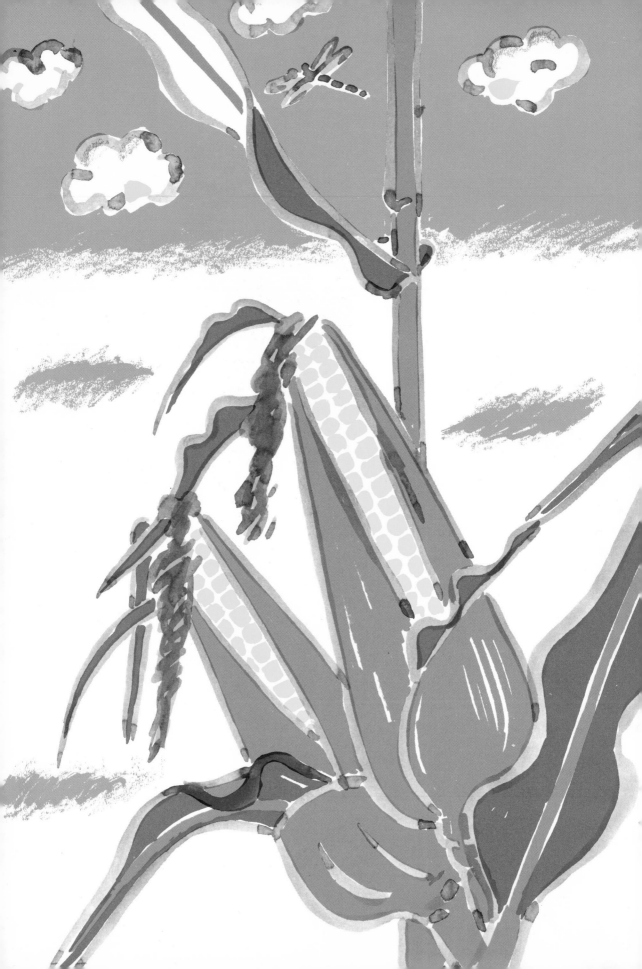

Sunset bakes the autumn sky.
The corn is ripe.
Popcorn pops out of the husks.

The sweet potatoes are plump.
They worked so hard.
"Hurry, dig us up," they sing.

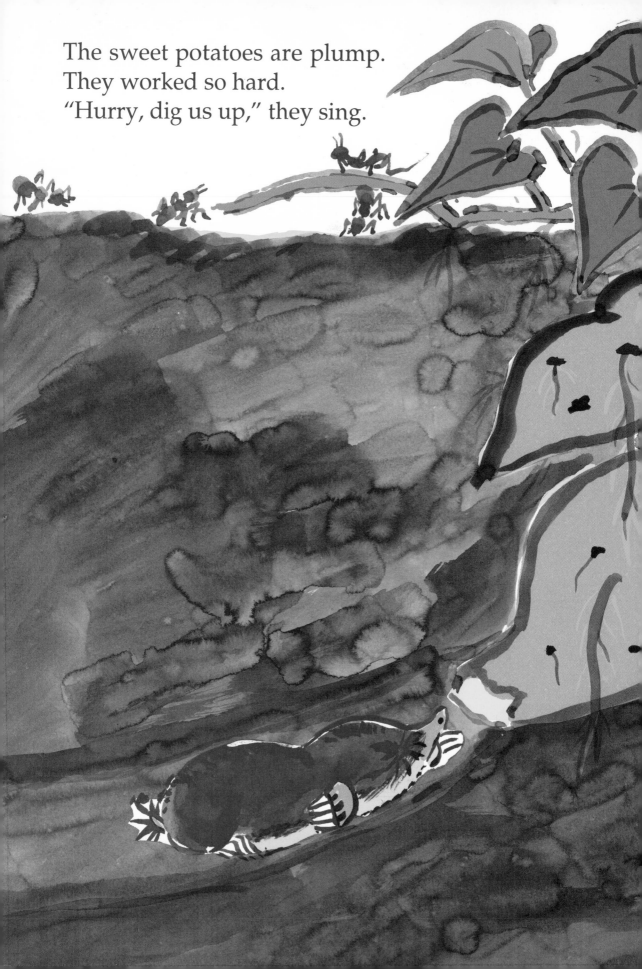

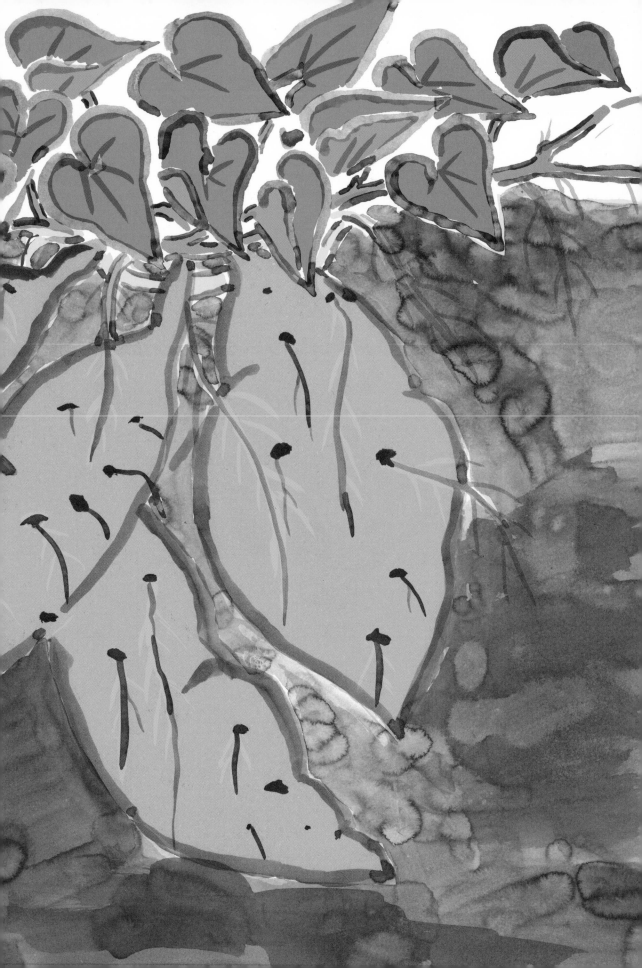

All winter long,
Roots stay in the garden.
"We don't mind the cold."

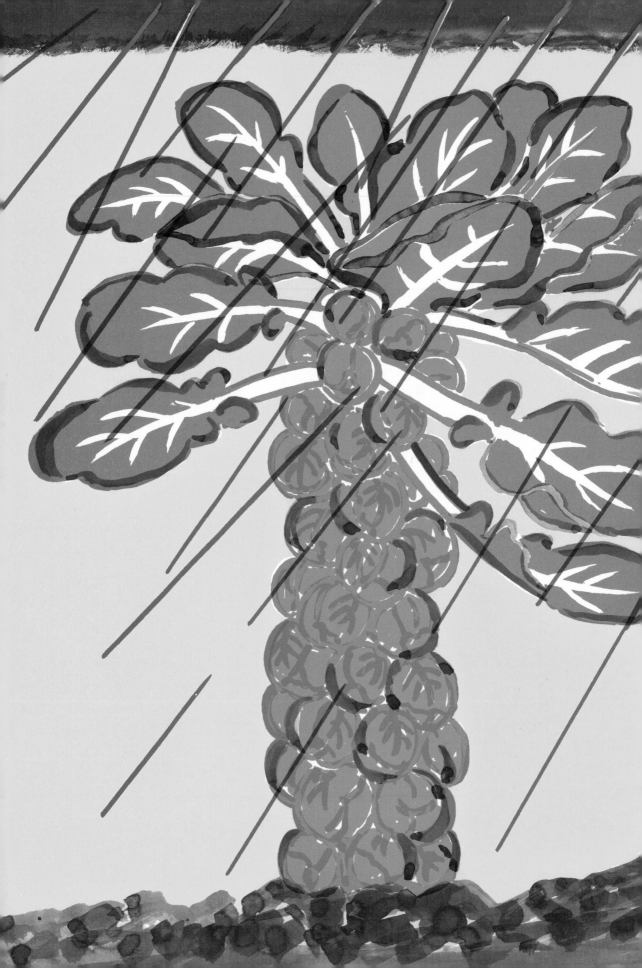

Broccoli and brussels sprouts,
Cousins in the ground.
Both love the winter rains
Pouring all around.

The cabbage is dreaming of seeds......seeds.....
Silver seeds in the sky become the universe.

Did you find the garden full of wonder?
Thank you, Mother Nature.
Thank you.

HAPPY VEGGIES, by Mayumi Oda

Copyright © 1986, by Mayumi Oda. All Rights Reserved. Printed in Japan.
Originally published in Japan as *Genki Na Yasaitachi*, by Koguma-sha.
English language translation © 1988, by Mayumi Oda. Worldwide English language
rights arranged with Koguma-sha through Japan Foreign-Rights Centre.
Published by Parallax Press, P.O. Box 7355, Berkeley, California 94707.
ISBN 0-938077-14-7